D1196714

RAVAN LOCAL HISTORY SERIES

THE SOWETO UPRISINGS:
Counter-memories of June 1976

Sifiso Mxolisi Ndlovu

RAVAN PRESS

Published by Ravan Press, 1998
PO Box 145 Randburg 2125 South Africa

© Sifiso Mxolisi Ndlovu 1998

Cover design and typesetting by KC Publishing Services

ISBN 0 86975 491 2

Printed and bound by CTP Book Printers, Cape

Dedication

Dedicated to the class of 1976: Form Twos, Phefeni Junior Secondary School, and my extended family, particularly Mkhulu.

Acknowledgements

Many thanks to Paul Ndaba, Njabulo Nkonyane and Hezekiel Khumalo for their contributions.

The publishers would also like to thank the Mayibuye Centre for the photographs and the *Sowetan* for permission to reproduce the newspaper articles from *The World*.

Acronyms used in this book

ANC   African National Congress
ATASA   African Teachers' Association of South Africa
AZAPO   Azanian People's Organisation
BC   Black Consciousness
BCM   Black Consciousness Movement
BPA   Black Parents' Association
BPC   Black People's Convention
PAC   Pan African Congress
PJSS   Phefeni Junior Secondary School
SASM   South African Students' Movement
SASO   South African Students' Organisation
SAYCO   South African Youth Congress
SSRC   Soweto Students' Representative Council
UBC   Urban Bantu Council
UDF   United Democratic Front

Note:

These are the years of schooling referred to in this book:
Form One: 8 years of schooling, the first year of high school
Form Two: 9 years of schooling, the second year of high school
Form Three: 10 years of schooling, the third year of high school etc

Introduction

What makes a place? What gives a place meaning? Each separate volume of the Local History Series focuses on a particular place in South Africa, which has been defined by a significant event or series of events, as recalled by or narrated to the author.

The series will be of interest to teachers, students, pupils and everyone who wants to know more about local history, to 'dig beneath the surface' and discover the memories and intimate, personal stories behind the official versions of history. It will provide primary sources of information – in contrast to the secondary sources prevalent in South African history textbooks – which will enable readers to formulate their own opinions about place and time in South African history.

The series editors, Luli Callinicos and Monica Seeber, believe we should develop historical skills by, when possible, listening to the voices of others, including those of ordinary men and women and understanding how events have touched their lives as well as our lives. The Local History Series aims to show how people's lives have shaped the places they live in and it uses existing knowledge and experience to facilitate the transition from what is known to what is still to be learned.

Luli Callinicos, author of the series *A People's History of South Africa* and 1988 recipient of the Noma Award for Publishing in Africa, has always been concerned about discovering history 'from below'. In her work on heritage, she is exploring how historical sites and places are given meaning by the experiences and memories of ordinary people.

Monica Seeber is fascinated by place and by the unrecorded histories of ordinary people which shape it. She conceptualised the Local History Series while working as a publisher and now works as a publishing consultant.

Police preparing to shoot at protesting schoolchildren, on 16 June 1976.

Part One: An eyewitness account

The mistake that the police made was to release the police dog – it injured one of our students. The students decided to kill the dog. When the dog was killed, the police then started to use live ammunition – we then ran away, helter-skelter, dispersing in all directions around Phefeni. Word came about that one student was killed, his name was Hector...

Paul Ndaba – December 1995

For us in the black community, the dog was a symbol of police power, brutality and of the contempt of white supremacists for black people's dignity and life. Most police dogs, and those privately owned by white South Africans are 'colour-conscious'. They are often trained to attack black people without restraint and to be venomous towards black people in general. The latter are often seen as unwanted intruders, invading white people's personal space and life.

The Soweto uprising was a turning point in our history. It exploded into a momentous event, leading to major repercussions that are still with us today. It reinvigorated the ailing African National Congress (ANC) as well as the Pan African Congress (PAC). It led to the re-examination of the Black Consciousness Movement (BCM). It aroused world abhorrence of apartheid's child killers and resulted in a dual response from the South African regime: further ruthless repression and ineffective reforms. It also left us

1

'World' car rushes shot school riot victim to clinic

ONE OF the gunshot victims of yesterday's bloody riot in Soweto was rushed to Phefeni Clinic in a WORLD Press car by WORLD reporter Sophie Tema, who witnessed the start of the riot.

But the journey to the clinic was in vain – the young boy who had been shot was already dead.

According to Miss Tema's eyewitness account, the riot started when police threw a teargas shell into a large crowd of school students who were taunting them.

Miss Tema was standing behind the police lines at the start of the riot.

A crowd of students which she estimated at "thousands" had gathered in front of Phefeni Junior Secondary School and were singing the Sotho national anthem, "Morena Boloka Sechaba Sa Heso", when about 10 police vehicles arrived.

Miss Tema said she estimated there were about 30 policemen, the majority of whom were Black. White police were armed with revolvers.

When police arrived a section of the crowd began taunting them and waving placards, while the remainder kept singing.

A White policeman then

> World reporter Sophie Tema was an eyewitness to yesterday's riot in Soweto in which at least six people died and 40 were injured. Here is her report.

hurled what seemed to be a teargas shell – which released a cloud of smoke or gas – into the crowd. Miss Tema did not get close enough to be affected by the gas and she did not see if any students were affected.

ANGRY

Miss Tema said the crowd immediately became angry and began throwing rocks and any other objects they could find at the police.

At no stage, she said, did police warn the students to disperse and there did not seem to be any communication at all between the crowd and the police.

Immediately the crowd began throwing rocks, Miss Tema said. She saw a White policeman pull out his revolver, point it and fire it. As soon as the shot was fired other policemen also began firing.

The students began running and she saw one student whom

she estimated to be about 20 or 21 years old, hit in the chest and fall. Other students took him to the nearby Phefeni clinic.

Small groups of students then kept running out of side streets from various directions and stoning the police before running away again. Miss Tema did not think this activity was organised, but was spontaneous.

She then saw a young boy whom she estimated to be between six and seven years old fall with a bullet wound.

"He had a bloody froth on his lips and he seemed to be seriously hurt so I took him to the Phefeni Clinic in a Press car but he was dead when we arrived," she said.

BLEEDING

On leaving the clinic Miss Tema was approached by a young man, not a student, who was bleeding from a wound in his thigh. He told her that he had felt a burning pain and realised he was bleeding. Miss Tema also took him to the clinic.

When she returned to the scene of the riot, Miss Tema said, shooting was still going on. She saw the body of a Black policeman lying on the ground covered with a sheet of paper.

Reporter of The World, Sophie Tema, provides a shocking eyewitness account of the bloody uprising of 16 June 1976.

17 June 1976 The World

2

with the insurmountable problem of the 'lost generation', the majority of whom are black. All this was triggered by the actions of a handful of schoolkids. How this all came about is what this book promises to reveal.

March and April 1976

In 1976, I was a 14-year-old Form Two student at Phefeni Junior Secondary School (PJSS). We were on a go-slow well before the official class boycott by Form One and Form Two students on 17 May 1976. From March onwards we dedicated the afternoon lessons in our class, from 2 o'clock to about 4 o'clock, to discussions about the directive that Afrikaans should be the medium of instruction in our school. Ours was one of the schools chosen where the pilot programme of this directive was to be implemented. It is worth noting that this only affected Forms One and Two. The senior students – that is, Form Three in our school and at high schools throughout Soweto – were excluded. These afternoon sessions were out of bounds for our prefects (except for one Seth Mazibuko), for teachers and other authorities including the principal, Mr Mpulo.

We were uncompromising about this matter. We told our teachers and certain other authorities that the major reason behind our action was that we received very disheartening feedback and low marks from the various subjects that used Afrikaans as a medium of instruction. Our class, Form Two A, supposedly had the best pupils in the school and we were therefore compelled to register for science subjects, as well as Mathematics.

It was a bitter experience for us in 1976 to study – for the first time in our lives in Afrikaans – Mathematics, Geography, Physical Science and Biology. This is because in the previous year we used English and in 1976 our marks dropped. One has to mention that during those days the slogan 'pass one pass all'[1] was unheard of.

3

WORLD
OUR OWN OUR ONLY PAPER

Phone Johannesburg
27-6081

FEBRUARY 25, 1976

Asking too much of our kids

WHETHER the South African Government likes it or not, many urban African parents are bitterly opposed to their children being forced to learn in Afrikaans.

We can well appreciate that this may be a sore point with a Government dedicated to propagating Afrikaans. But the objection of these parents is well founded.

They believe that it is demanding too much of their children to expect them to learn in their home tongue, English AND Afrikaans. After all, White pupils, with all the educational advantages they enjoy,

are not forced to adopt an African language as a third medium of instruction.

But whatever the merits of the case, we were astounded to note that Black school boards have been summarily warned to keep off this issue.

Top Department of Bantu Education officials have explained that this is a professional matter which does not fall within the orbit of our school boards!

Their argument is that the medium of instruction is a matter of policy laid down 13 years ago by the Minister of Bantu Education and only he can affect a change.

Our reply to this is that it only shows how out of date the Minister and his Department must be.

God-like decisions by White officials – even Cabinet ministers – on matters of vital importance to Blacks are just not good enough. The old dictum that Whites know what is best for Blacks is no longer acceptable.

As for school boards, their exact functions is not the point at issue. It is the principle of Black parents deciding what is best for their children.

And the Government listening to them.

'The old dictum that whites know what is best for blacks is no longer acceptable.' Black parents are bitterly opposed to Afrikaans as medium of instruction.

The World 25 Feb 76

4

Meeting on schools language issue

THE Meadowlands Tswana School Board, which resigned last month over the enforced use of Afrikaans as a medium of instruction in schools, is to hold a public meeting on the controversial directive this Sunday.

The meeting is scheduled for 9 a.m. at the Thutolore Secondary School in Meadowlands and it will be addressed by the members who resigned from the local Tswana School Board.

The language issue is still causing confusion and frustration in some Soweto schools.

Following a meeting between Chief Mangope of BophuthaTswana and the South African Government, the homeland leader told the Tswana school boards that they were free to choose their medium of instruction in their schools in consultation with the Department of Bantu Education.

This seems to contradict the ruling that has been given by the regional office of Bantu Education in Johannesburg that both mathematics and social studies be given in Afrikaans.

At the same time, schools may still apply for exemption on the grounds that they do not have teachers qualified to teach in Afrikaans.

However, classes must continue with the dual medium until the Department of Bantu Education has investigated the situation, one principal said.

'CONFUSED'

"Here we are already into March and I am utterly confused about what to do," said the Principal, who heads a higher primary school which has a Form One class.

"I am applying for exemption from the Afrikaans rule because my teachers just are not qualified to teach in this language.

"As for the children – I have seen how some of them are struggling with English. To have Afrikaans on top of this is just too much."

Although most of the school boards have capitulated to the medium of instruction directive from the Department of Bantu Education, the teachers and principals are very dissatisfied.

Members of the Meadowlands Tswana school board resign and call for a meeting to discuss the use of Afrikaans as medium of instruction.

The World   5 March 1976

5

Parents stand firm in language row

By Don Manaka

MEADOWLANDS parents have stood by their decision of rejecting Afrikaans as a medium of instruction in their schools and have asked the BophuthaTswana Government to pursue the matter further with the South African Government.

This was after hearing a report of talks between the Bophuthatswana Government and the South African Prime Minister, Mr B J Vorster, at a heated meeting at Thutolore Secondary School, Zone One, Meadowlands, yesterday.

CIRCULAR

They asked the Tswana Urban Representative, Mr S L L Rathebe, to ask the Bophuthatswana Government to take the matter further with the Central Government.

They said in the meantime a circular issued by the Tswana School Board in January that the Tswana children should be taught through the medium of English should stand.

The Bophuthatswana Government took up the question of the medium of instruction in Meadow-lands with the Central Government after the chairman of the Meadowlands Tswana School Board, Mr J M Peele and the former chairman, Mr A A Letlape were expelled. Shortly thereafter the entire Meadowlands School Board resigned.

Mrs Elizabeth Mathope: "If we allow our children to be taught in Afrikaans all they can become is ministers of the Dutch Reformed Church."

Mrs Elizabeth Mathope told the meeting: "We pay for the education of our children and we should determine their education."

Black parents speak out at a heated meeting: 'We pay for the education of our children and we should determine their education.' The World 8 March 1976

We welcomed the highly competitive spirit and conscientiousness that existed in this class of 1975-1976. We knew from our tests, exams and other forms of assessment, that we were a highly efficient and successful class.

During these formative days of the uprisings we discussed student issues only – issues that affected us directly in the school

6

and classroom. This included authoritarianism and the absence of channels, through which we could talk to the inspectorate and other relevant officials of the regional department of Bantu Education or through which we could seek redress for our grievances. We held several unsuccessful meetings with our prefects, teachers, principal and a junior representative from the regional office. As early as February and March, leading local, black newspapers and some parents and teachers, were, like us, very concerned about using Afrikaans as a medium of instruction in black schools.

May 1976

I do not remember any liberation movement, such as the Black Consciousness Movement or the South African Student Movement (SASM) contributing to our daily meetings and discussions. In short, as students we faced our destiny and problems. After a month or two on a go-slow with no solution in sight, we decided to embark on an official class boycott which commenced in mid-May. As the Joe's Burg column in *The World* newspaper correctly pointed out, Afrikaans as a medium of instruction was 'a killer subject'.

We had to use unorthodox methods to convince our teachers and principal that we were serious. I remember one incident when we dumped various Maths, Geography and Biology textbooks written in Afrikaans, at our principal's office and when he emerged from the pile at his door. The incident was comical. I could not help laughing. A few days later, other schools in the vicinity decided to join us. These included Belle Higher Primary Schools in which the Standard Five pupils were affected by the directive of using Afrikaans as a medium of instruction. But some of these schools soon returned to class after being sweet-talked by various authorities.

Continued on page 12

7

Now I know why teachers want to get out

JOE'S BURG

I HAVE BEEN wondering why so many of my friends in the teaching profession have been phoning me desperately asking me to let them know if I heard of a clerical position somewhere.

After a closer look at the latest directive from the Department of Black Education I can appreciate the frustrations of these ladies and gentlemen!

According to a teacher in this burg – one of the many who are threatening to resign and join industry – the department is pushing Afrikaans down their throats, expecting secondary schools to teach 50 percent of their subjects in Afrikaans.

AFRIKAANS

"You just look at the Junior Certificate and Matriculation results and you don't have to look far to realise that Afrikaans is the killer subject. And the principals can tell you what a sweat it is to get teachers willing to offer Afrikaans, let alone being capable and qualified to teach it," said the teacher.

The situation is really bad when one considers the decision by members of the Meadowlands Tswana School Board to resign en bloc.

And if I know old man Letlape and the determined Mr Joe Peele, both executives of the Meadowlands board, they really mean business when they say they have the full backing of all the Tswana boards. And the department will be faced with a serious situation if the parents come up and elect the same men onto the boards. It could go on and on and in the end it is the poor students who are going to suffer!

FIRM STAND

While I am fully behind the Meadowlands board for their firm stand in refusing to have their students do half their subjects in Afrikaans and the other half in English, I would also like to sound a word of advice to the members of the boards.

If you expect any co-operation from the teachers you must also assist them when you are still in power. Far too many school board members tend to bully teachers and boast that they are the bosses. This is one time that you should effectively stand together.

And just to give you an idea of how Mathematics would sound in Afrikaans here we go: "Die loodregte lyn is die kortste van al dwarslyne wat kan geteken word vanaf buite 'n genoemde dwarslyn."

Frustrated black teachers start looking for jobs outside of education, as they are forced to teach in Afrikaans.

The World   13 Feb 1976

8

School strike over

Hundreds of kids return to classes this morning

THE STRIKE by more than 2 000 Soweto pupils which started with one Orlando West school almost three weeks ago and spread to another six schools, is virtually over today.

Pupils from Belle, Thulasizwe and Pimville Bantu Higher Primaries are back in class today while at least half the striking pupils at Emthonjeni Higher Primary have returned.

By this morning it was only the form one and two pupils at Phefeni Junior Secondary who were still remaining out of class.

Pupils at the Senaoane Junior Secondary who were the latest to join the strike this week were unsure of whether to return to class or not early today.

Pupils at the seventh school in Diepkloof who joined the strike last week are also back at school today.

Although the Emthonjeni and Belle pupils have returned to class they seem to have won a minor victory.

It is reported by the pupils that they have gained the assurance that both mathematics and social studies – the two subjects taught in Afrikaans which led to the strike – will be suspended for the present.

The principal of Thulasizwe Higher Primary School, Mr L Mguni, said yesterday that he was happy that at least the students were learning, even if they had dropped some subjects.

"They are now doing only five subjects but it's better than nothing," he said.

He said this was the result of a meeting with pupils where they were convinced to go back to classes as the June examinations were about to start.

Meanwhile it has been reported that the controversy will have a sequel in Parliament tomorrow, when Mr M C Botha, Minister of Bantu Education, is to answer a series of questions from Dr Alex Boraine, MP, of the Progressive Reform party.

The questions will be based on the background to the strike and whether the matter is receiving attention from the Government.

Striking students return to class on condition
that Maths and Social studies classes
taught in Afrikaans are suspended.

The World   3 June 1976

9

The route of the Soweto march

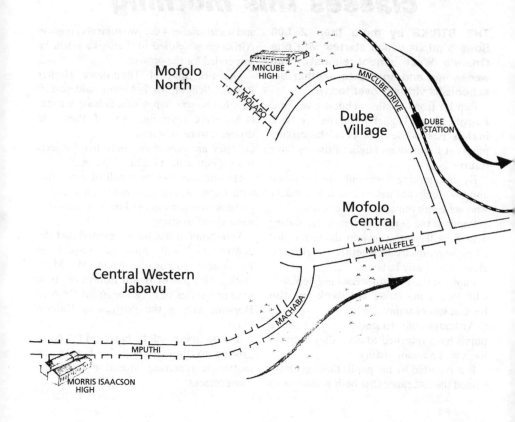

Mofolo North

MNCUBE HIGH

MNCUBE DRIVE

MOFOLO

Dube Village

DUBE STATION

Mofolo Central

MAHALEFELE

Central Western Jabavu

MACHABA

MPUTHI

MORRIS ISAACSON HIGH

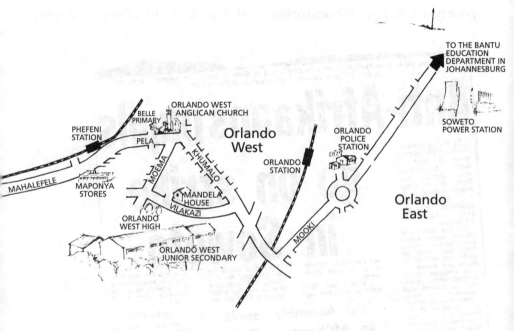

11

In our school, however, we were determined to carry on with the class boycott. In fact for me, this was the last time in my life I went into a classroom in Soweto or any other school that was controlled by the South African state. The reason we were so determined was that we had first-hand experience of the conditions inside the classrooms. In 1975, while we were using English as a medium of instruction, we had to be satisfied with poorly–equipped laboratories and the lack of other necessary

Some of the pupils from Phefeni Junior Secondary School in Orlando West, who yesterday demonstrated against Afrikaans as medium of instruction at their school.

Anti-Afrikaans pupils go on strike in Soweto

By Willie Bokala

STUDENTS threatened to beat up their headmaster and threw textbooks out of classroom windows in a demonstration against being taught some subjects in Afrikaans.

The 600 students at Phefeni Junior Secondary School, Orlando West, then went on strike and refused to attend any classes.

In a violent display of pupil-power yesterday the students also demanded the re-instatement of Mr Mahlangu, chairman of the school board, whom they claimed had been sacked because he was against using Afrikaans for teaching.

The demonstration started after morning assembly when students from Form One

and Form Two refused to go to their classrooms.

A teacher told THE WORLD that when the students were asked to go to their classrooms they started shouting. Some let down the tyres of the principal's car.

They then confronted the principal, Mr S C Mpulo, and demanded that he call the school inspector. They said the inspector should come and explain why difficult subjects were taught in Afrikaans. The principal was threatened by students,

who told him that if he was not back within a few minutes with the inspector, they would beat him up.

APPROACHED

The teacher said the head went away and when he came back he told the students that the inspector had refused to come.

When approached by reporters yesterday, Mr Mpulo refused to talk about the controversy.

'Kei Assembly moves on Afrikaans — P 16

The World 18 May 1976

Pupils threaten to beat up their principal for allegedly sacking the school board's chair because he protested against Afrikaans for teaching.

12

KIDS KEEP UP STRIKE
Big march planned

THE STRIKE by pupils of Phefeni Junior Secondary School, in Orlando West, Soweto, against the enforced use of Afrikaans in their school, entered its third day today against a background of mounting violence.

The students are now planning to march to their school board offices at Diepkloof.

The decision came at a meeting the students held this morning in the school yard as they continued to boycott classes until their demands that they be taught mathematics and social studies in English have been met.

They also selected an interim committee to meet the principal, Mr Charles Mpulo, and the staff. They said they would wait for a report back from their committee and thereafter march to the school board to meet the chairman.

Violent

The strike took a violent new turn yesterday when they seized a tape recorder from the vice-principal, Mr F Nhlapo, accused him of being a police informer and threatened to beat him up.

When the new school board chairman, Mr Ngwenya, failed to turn up to address the students as he was expected to do, they began stoning the principal's office and classrooms.

Other students and teachers had to run for cover when the stone throwing demonstration broke out.

Mr Nhlapo had to be escorted home by the principal, Mr Charles Mpulo, when students threatened to beat him up.

The strike started on Monday when students refused to go to classes in protest at some subjects being taught in Afrikaans.

They threatened the headmaster and threw out Afrikaans textbooks.

Yesterday, Mr Mpulo ordered students home when they again refused recorder, and accused him of being a police informer.

The stone-throwing stopped when the principal told the students that the school-board chairman refused to talk to them and had said that the principal should talk to them.

"I have had discussions with the chairman in my office and he had told me that if you don't want to listen to me, he will not talk to you. We, me and the teachers, side with you. We are trying our best but we are failing," Mr Mpulo said.

The principal of Orlando West Junior Secondary School, Mr Charles Mpulo, talks to students yesterday at his trouble-torn school.

1600 pupils keep up strike

THE 1 600 striking Soweto schoolchildren today defied their parents who at a weekend meeting in Orlando West decided they should return to school. The pupils, from four Orlando East schools, again refused to go into class this morning.

The pupils are from Phefeni Junior Secondary (form one and two), and the Standard five and form one pupils at Belle, Thulasizwe and Emthonjeni Higher Primary Schools.

They began their strike last week in protest at having to study mathematics and social studies through Afrikaans.

MILLING

Early today the striking pupils were milling around their schools in Orlando but would not go into class.

At a packed parents' meeting in the township over the weekend it was decided that the pupils should return to school while the whole matter is being looked into.

Last week the circuit inspector of Bantu Education, Mr M C De Beer, said he was taking no action against the striking pupils because he was "in no position to force the pupils" to go to school.

At a packed meeting, parents decide pupils should go back to school but now about 1 600 pupils defy them and continue their strike.

24 May 1976 The World

resources and facilities. But the use of Afrikaans the following year as a medium of instruction soon compounded the issues. What were initially problems that related to the lack of facilities and resources, now became epistemological and ideological issues which included the (ab)use of language and power. As we were not benefiting from this situation, we asked ourselves: 'What is the use of studying something that does not make sense to you, does not sustain your quest for knowledge and does not improve your critical faculties?' According to me these are classroom issues and they needed people with first-hand experience to articulate them; hence our determination to use passive resistance as a tool to put our grievances to the authorities.

One has to also point out the problematic manner in which the terms 'student' or 'pupil' are used when discussing the origins of the uprisings. These terms are used simplistically, in a way that does not highlight

14

and take into cognisance the various differences among us. We were not a homogeneous group. Students from the various high schools in Soweto were not at first interested in our plight and struggle, as they were using English as a medium of instruction. They carried on with their studies as if nothing was happening during the formative, crucial days leading to the uprisings. I remember that in my school the senior students, Form Three (Std Eights), were both aloof and dismissive towards us. The Form Four and Form Five students from our high school and our neighbours, Orlando West High (popularly known as Matseke) were equally uninterested. The majority of the senior students were very reactionary and perceived us as young upstarts and delinquents who were interfering and disturbing 'normal' schooling. Therefore like the Tsietsies[2] of those early days, they simply went on with their studies in March, April, May and early June 1976 without questioning the status quo.

To elaborate, one should note that during the early period, that is prior to June, the student leaders that later emerged – like Tsietsie Mashinini, Khotso Seathlolo, Dan Montsitsi, Murphy Morobe and representatives of South African Students' Movement – were not involved in our struggle. This is because they were senior high school students who were not affected. They were exempted by the Ministry of Bantu Education from the 'Afrikaans as medium' directive. They were among the last group using English as a medium of instruction in black secondary and high schools. Furthermore, historical fiction films such as *Sarafina* and *Cry Freedom* and other media wrongly assume that the students of Morris Isaacson High School in Central Western Jabavu played a crucial role in events leading up to 16 June 1976. This is because the dominant leaders of Soweto Students' Representative Council (SSRC) were from this high school, including its first president Tsietsie Mashinini[3]. This representation is not correct. The SSRC was formed early in

15

Pupils form new body

SOWETO high and secondary school students have formed a new body – the Soweto Students' Representative Council – to represent their interests.

The chairman of the new group is Tsietsie Mashinini, of Morris Isaacson High School, Soweto.

The new body was formed at a special meeting at Morris Isaacson High School yesterday. It was attended by more than 40 student delegates from Soweto high and secondary schools.

At the same time the meeting condemned the burning of schools and other institutions by arsonists and urged students to return to school.

MEMORANDUM

The meeting also decided to draw up a memorandum which will be presented to the Black Parents' Association, which they consider the only relevant parent body, for the association to present to the authorities. The memorandum will demand the release of all people detained as a result of the recent disturbances.

The Soweto Urban Bantu Council was condemned by the students, who later declared it a 'stooge body'. The UBC was criticised for going to Pretoria to meet the Minister of Bantu Education, Mr M C Botha, without having been given a mandate by the 'people.'

In a statement after the meeting, Tsietsie Mashinini of Morris Isaacson, who chaired the meeting, said the students condemned the action of arsonists who were going around burning schools and other valuable buildings.

"We are also aware that there is a group of students who go around schools trying to organise other boycotts. We want to discourage this as it will only stir more confusion," he said.

Referring to students who on Sunday called for the Minister of Justice, Mr Jimmy Kruger to meet Soweto students at Jabulani within the next two weeks, Tsietsie said they were trying to impress people.

"When things are like this, it is not for us to go all out and organise confusion. We should rather come together. Students' behaviour at Jabulani was uncalled for," he said.

It was also suspected that most students who were at Jabulani on Sunday were not local, he said.

Issues raised by the students at yesterday's meeting included:

- An appeal to Soweto parents to do something about the continual arrest of students.
- An appeal for students to go back to school to be able to solve their problems.
- A call for the Bantu Education system to be scrapped as it only helped in domesticating Blacks to make them tools of the racist regime.
- Condemnation of the UBC as not representing the people as just a "puppet body".

The newly formed council will hold periodical meetings at which progress will be reported.

At a meeting of over 40 delegates, Soweto students set up the Soweto Students' Representative Council, headed by Tsietsie Mashinini.

3 August 1976. The World

16

August 1976, one and a half months after the actual day of protest in June. Therefore its formation was influenced by the events that took place before and after 16 June 1976.

16 June 1976

Unfortunately, to get the senior students to take us seriously, we had to use force during the first week of June. This led to the abandonment of the Form Three half-yearly examinations (and those that were taking place at Matseke too). We were unyielding and uncompromising. As early as June 1976, the press portrayed our determination lucidly when other schools joined us in class boycotts.

It was after this period that we were able to speak with one voice as students; and this move was not achieved through the efforts of the SASM or any

Although parents encourage children to go back to school the number of striking pupils rises to about 2 700.

1 June 1976 The World

Seventh school joins strike

By Willie Bokala

ALTHOUGH parents are reported to be trying their best to end the Afrikaans language boycott in Soweto schools, a seventh school joined the strike to bring the number of striking schoolchildren to about 2 700, this morning.

The latest school to be hit by the controversy is Senaoane Junior Secondary School in Soweto, where about 600 pupils involving form ones, twos and threes, refused to go to classes after assembly.

The principal of the school, Mr N E Nzimande, said he met a few top students who told him they had decided to down books because their plea for a change in the medium of instruction had not been met.

The students said they wanted to see Mr M C de Beer, the school inspector, or the chairman of the school board.

When asked about the strike one of the students

✖ To Back Page

17

Questions in Parliament

School strike: Botha quizzed

THE STRIKE of more than 1 500 Soweto schoolchildren in protest at being forced to study in Afrikaans will have its sequel in Parliament on Friday.

The Progressive Reform Party spokesman on Bantu Education, Dr Alex Boraine, is to ask the Minister, Mr M C Botha, a series of questions of the scope and background to the strike.

He will also ask what Government plans have resulted from it.

To establish the facts of the occurrence, Dr Boraine has asked whether pupils of any Soweto schools have recently refused to attend classes, which schools were affected, how many pupils normally attended the schools and what the reasons were for their non-attendance.

He then goes on to ask what steps are being taken in the matter by the Department of Bantu Education.

There has long been simmering dissatisfaction in Soweto over the Government's policy of using

Afrikaans and English on a 50-50 basis as the medium of instruction in Black schools.

Although the department has indicated its willingness to be flexible where teachers are not proficient to teach in both languages, the application of the policy nevertheless resulted in a protest strike against the use of Afrikaans as the medium of instruction in the schools concerned.

The strike which now affects five Soweto schools is in its second week and show little sign of ending.

In the second week of the strike, Dr Alex Boraine plans to quiz the Minister of Bantu Education about what steps he will be taking to deal with the crisis!

liberation movement. Subsequently all the secondary and high schools in Soweto became part of the process. A day of protest action was agreed upon – 16 June. On the eve of the big march planned by these schools, 15 June 1976, *The World* newspaper proclaimed: 'Language strike continues'.

Language strike continues

by COLIN NXUMALO

THE AFRIKAANS language boycott, which at one stage affected seven Soweto schools, has now gone into its fifth week – with three schools still on strike.

There appears to be no immediate solution for getting the outstanding 300 students who are on strike back to class before the end of the half-year school term.

DEPUTATION

Schools whose students are still on strike are: Phefeni Junior Secondary, Belle Higher Primary School and Emthonjeni Higher Primary School, all in Orlando.

Students at Belle sent a deputation to the principal yesterday morning to find out if their demands, that the medium of instruction be changed to English, have been met.

When they were told that the matter was still under consideration, they left their classes and went home.

It is understood that those who have gone back to classes at the other schools which were also affected, have refused to write Social Studies and Mathematics – the subjects taught in Afrikaans.

Five weeks into the strike, pupils find out that their concerns are still under consideration. The strike continues.

The World 15 June 1976

Verbatim statement of Paul Ndaba – December 1995 [Mr Ndaba was my classmate at PJSS in 1976. He was 17 years old then. Paul Ndaba has been employed at Standard Bank since finishing his matric in the early 1980s.]

February and March 1976

When we passed our Form One going into Form Two, the school principal, Mr Mpulo, addressed all the Form Twos at the beginning of the year (1976) that from henceforth the students in Form Two were going to do Maths, History and Biology in Afrikaans. We did not know what was coming. We sort of accepted – we did not delve into the practicalities. We got our textbooks and tuition began. But I tell you it was a hell of a problem. Then we went back to the teachers and we tried to set up a meeting with the principal trying to highlight this problem [of using Afrikaans as a medium of instruction]...

Firstly the language itself was a problem, you would get a word in Mathematics being said in

19

Afrikaans, like 'algebra', and this word in Afrikaans is a word I cannot even understand. You come to Biology, Geography... all those words. The words for the instruments that we had to use [in the lab] were just not on. Those words were just difficult. Secondly, the teachers themselves were not well equipped to teach these subjects in Afrikaans. They were just able to teach Afrikaans as a language [including literature and poetry]. The textbooks in this respect were user-friendly for them but not those they had to use to teach Maths, Geography and Biology... The marks that we got when we did all these three subjects in Afrikaans were extremely bad. We saw that we were not getting anywhere.

The World 11 Feb 1976

'School sackings will not lead to withdrawals'

MR W C Ackerman, regional director of Bantu Education in the Southern Transvaal, says he does not think his dismissal of two Tswana schoolboard executives will lead to a mass withdrawal of school children from Meadowlands school.

He was reacting to a report that the sacking of Mr Joseph Peele and Mr Abner Letlape, both executives of the Tswana Board, has caused parents to show support for their board by a massive withdrawal of their children from Meadowlands schools.

REASONS

He was surprised to hear that parents objected to their dismissal when schoolboard regulations clearly empower "the regional director to

dismiss any member of the board at any time and for whatever reason as he may deem fit."

When THE WORLD asked him for reasons that led to the executives' sacking he snapped back: "You should not think I am foolish enough to disclose the reasons. In terms of the regulations reasons cannot be disclosed."

There was no confirmation that the meeting, at which the withdrawal threats were made by parents, was actually held.

Teachers and parents who spoke to THE WORLD denied any knowledge of the alleged action. They also expressed surprise at the report that they intended drawing their children from schools if the two men were not reinstated in their positions.

When a regional director of Bantu Education sacks two Tswana school board executives,

he is surprised to hear that parents wish to take their children out of school.

20

To elaborate on Paul's comments, it is useful to highlight here that early in February the entire Meadowlands school board was sacked by the dictatorial regional department of Bantu Education for taking a stand against the use of Afrikaans as medium of instruction. They had the same misgivings as the students at PJSS. Paul continues:

It was best for us to revert back to [using] English as a medium of instruction... We pressed on the matter with the principal and teachers. We started being very much negative... We approached the principal who promised us that he will go and see the regional inspector who was Mr De Beer. We then said to the principal we want this to be done as soon as possible. If it was possible he can come with Mr De Beer to address us... It was the month of March when the principal decided to take up the matter... The response from the inspectorate was not positive, that was during the first week of March... [Subsequently] what we decided to do was to stage a class boycott [in May] within the school yard itself and that was only involving the Form Twos.

It is apparent from Paul's evidence above that both the principal of PJSS and the school board (as stakeholders which governed this school on behalf of Bantu Education Ministry) were powerless, a poignant point which was later highlighted by one of the editorials of *The World* newspaper: 'The school boards are toothless'.

Continued on page 25

WEEKEND WORLD, Sunday, March 14, 1976

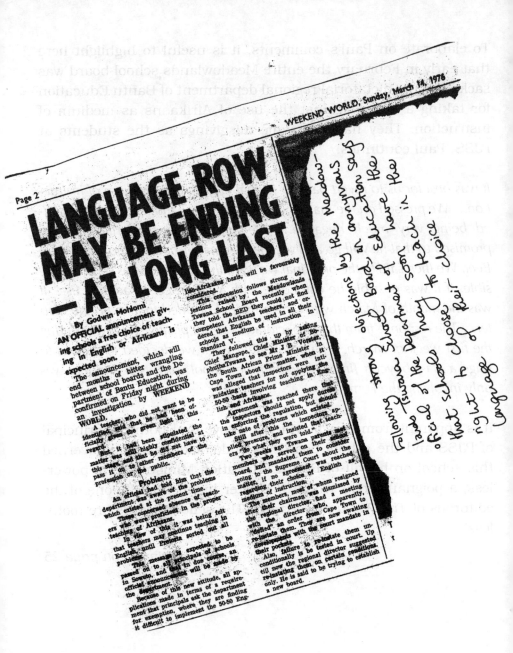

LANGUAGE ROW MAY BE ENDING — AT LONG LAST

By Godwin Mohlomi

AN OFFICIAL announcement giving schools a free choice of teaching in English or Afrikaans is expected soon.

The announcement, which will end months of bitter wrangling between school boards and the Department of Bantu Education, was confirmed on Friday night during an investigation by WEEKEND WORLD.

A teacher, who did not want to be identified, said that he had been officially given the green light in this regard.

But, it has been stipulated the matter was still highly confidential at this stage, and that he did not have to pass it on to other members of the profession or the public.

Problems

An official had told him that the department was aware of the problems which existed at the present time.

These concerned the absence of teachers who were proficient in the proper teaching of Afrikaans.

In view of this, it was being felt that teachers may continue teaching in English, until Pretoria sorted out all problems.

This message is expected to be passed on to all principals of schools in Soweto, and that in due course, an official announcement will be made by the department.

Because of this new attitude, all applications made in terms of a requirement that principals ask the department for exemption, where they are finding it difficult to implement the 50-50 English-Afrikaans basis, will be favourably considered.

This concession follows strong objections raised by the Meadowlands Tswana School Board recently when they told the BED they could not find competent Afrikaans teachers, and ordered that English be used in all their schools as medium of instruction in Standard V.

They followed this up by asking Chief Mangope, Chief Minister of BophuthaTswana to see Mr J B Vorster, the South African Prime Minister in Cape Town about the matter, when it was alleged that inspectors were intimidating teachers for not applying the 50-50 basis involving teaching in English and Afrikaans.

Agreement was reached there that the inspectors should not apply during the enforcing the regulation, but should take note of problems which existed.

Still after this the inspectors applied pressure, and insisted that teachers do what they were told.

Two weeks ago Tswana parents and members who served on their school board, and mandated them to consider going to the Supreme Court about the matter, if no agreement was reached regarding their choice of English as medium of instruction.

The members, most of whom resigned after their chairman had a meeting with the regional director, had a meeting with the director who, apparently, "defied" an order from Cape Town to re-instate them. They are now awaiting developments with the court mandate in their pockets.

Also, failure to re-instate them unconditionally be tested in court. Up till now the regional director suggested re-instating them on certain conditions only. He is said to be trying to establish a new board.

Following strong objections by the Meadows— board an anonymous says that school board of education soon in the land Tswana school may teach in the oficial of the Department have the that schools to choose their choice. right to choose their language

THE WORLD

OUR OWN, OUR ONLY PAPER

Telephone 27-6081 Johannesburg

The school boards are toothless

THE strikes by some Soweto students over the use of Afrikaans as a medium of instruction are growing to alarming proportions.

While we do not dismiss the claims of the students that they are being frustrated by the insistence on Afrikaans, we do believe that it is the duty of parents to protest against this move rather than the students, who should get on with their studies.

There have been accusations and counter-accusations while the strike has been going on. Tape recorders were seized by students because of feelings that a vice-principal was an "informer." The vice-principal himself has accused a teacher of having incited the kids into seizing the recorder. And all the time, students are wasting valuable time.

The students point out that they have expressed the desire to use English as medium of instruction, and nothing has been done. This, they claim, is why "Pupil Power" took over. Is this not, perhaps, a reflection on school boards, committees and parent associations?

Surely the parents, who pay hard-earned money to keep their kids at school, must have a strong voice in determining the future of their children?

But all these bodies are toothless. The final decision as to which language should be used as medium of instruction comes from the Department of Bantu Education. And the Department is not likely to apply their "deviation" principle lightly.

As Dr A P Treurnich, Deputy Minister of Bantu Administration and Education, said: Medium of instruction is a "professional matter" which should go to the principal, to the inspector, regional director and finally to the Department.

Nowhere is any mention made of parents, school committees and school boards.

THE WORLD

OUR OWN, OUR ONLY PAPER

A new deal?

ALTHOUGH we would very much like to be as optimistic as the African Teachers' Association of South Africa over discussions they held with the Department of Bantu Education, past experience has taught us to be wary of all "new deals" from the South African Government.

We have, in the past, pointed out the need for schools to use English as a medium of instruction because there are not enough teachers qualified to teach most subjects in Afrikaans. We have also pointed out that most of the books on subjects like history, mathematics, and the sciences, have been written in English.

But the Government has stood firm on its decision that the schools should use Afrikaans and English on a fifty-fifty basis. ATASA, following representation to education authorities, have now been promised a "new deal". We'll wait and see.

On meeting with the Department of Bantu Education, the African Teachers' Association is promised a 'new deal'.

Despite mass protest from pupils, parents and school boards, the Deputy Minister of Bantu Administration and Education says that the medium of instruction is a 'professional matter'.

23

Leaders lash 'stupid' education system

By
MOTHOBI MUTLOATSE

THIS WEEK'S strike by Soweto schoolchildren over the teaching of mathematics and science in Afrikaans was significant in that it had exposed the "stupidity" of Black education.

This was the view of Soweto UBC member Mr Leonard Mosala and veteran educationist Mr W B Ngakane now attached to the South African Council of Churches' technical bursaries department.

The strike by about 1 500 pupils from five schools was sparked off on Monday morning by students at Phefeni Junior Secondary School. They boycotted classes because mathematics and science were being taught in Afrikaans.

However, Mr M C de Beer, circuit inspector of the Department of Education, said the department was "doing nothing about the matter".

He said his office was not in a position to compel the pupils to return to classes.

At the time of going to Press, it was not known whether the strike would be called off.

Mr Ngakane said: "The strike exposed the stupidity of Bantu Education officials trying to reclaim lost opportunities.

"With legislation, the Afrikaner has created an attitude of hate on the part of the Black man. To think that a person who hates you can love your language, is to be stupid.

"We, as Blacks, have a right to create our own cultural organisations. We have the right to choose the medium of instruction for our children."

He added: "By forcing Black children to learn maths and science in Afrikaans, the authorities are giving Black pupils their first lesson in solidarity."

Mr Mosala said: "This week's pupil strike is significant in several ways.

"Firstly, it highlights the classroom problems encountered by both the teacher and the scholar. Secondly, it highlights the effects the use of Afrikaans has had over the years on the results of Black pupils.

"The manner in which Afrikaans is imposed on them makes it difficult for Black pupils to accept it willingly. The fault lies with the policy.

"The department should reconsider its indiscriminate enforcement of the use of Afrikaans in Black schools.

"Unless something is done quickly, this week's strike may spread to other parts of the country."

● The Secretary for Bantu Education, Mr G J Roussouw, is believed to be in Cape Town. No reasons were given for his trip.

At the onset of the strike, black leaders speak out: 'By forcing black children to learn Afrikaans the authorities are giving black pupils their first lesson in solidarity.'

23 May 1976, The World

24

May 1976

It was on a Friday afternoon and we made a declaration that as from the next week, Monday, we were not going to classes. Obviously the principal was going to ask us why, we were going to tell him we are on a class boycott... The Form Threes' medium of instruction was English. This directive [of using Afrikaans] was going to apply only to the Form Twos, that particular year. I do not know what was the situation in other junior secondaries then, but we had picked up the problem and we were prepared to fight it... The Form Threes did not know what was happening when we had a meeting that Friday [to decide about the class boycott]. They were not in the meeting and they were not informed and they were just amazed as to why we were not going into class [the next Monday]. They came during short break to ask us why and we told them we had staged a class boycott because of Afrikaans as a medium of instruction. In our meeting again we resolved not to include the Form Threes because they were not affected by the new system... They were never party at all to these class boycotts.

And after the whole week not going to class [Seth Mazibuko] came to us and said we should at least teach ourselves, try to get English textbooks and teach ourselves, and on the other hand stick to this boycott of Afrikaans as a medium of instruction... We did not want any teachers to come and teach us and we would teach ourselves in English up until Mr De Beer has decided to come and address our problem... As far as I can remember he never came... Since we carried this boycott in a disciplined manner, I would say that we were always in the school yard and then we would be in the class [during the actual boycott] from the morning up until 12 [teaching ourselves in English]. From then we would dismiss but we would still be inside the yard of the school [as we were supposed to knock off after 3 pm]. We had a sister school in Orlando East where our Form One students were accommodated, those students also joined us – we heard rumours that other schools have also joined, for example Belle Higher Primary School, kwa-Mahlobo Junior Secondary School in Meadowlands and other schools in Mzimhlophe and Klipspruit.

25

Strike school in deadlock

By Willie Bokala

THE STRIKE at Orlando West Junior Secondary School was no closer to ending last night. School officials tried desperately to get the children back into their classrooms – while the strike spread to another Soweto school.

In a series of attempts to end the deadlock – over the use of Afrikaans for teaching certain subjects – headmaster Mr Charles Mpulo met a students' committee, school committee chairman Mr Mkhize spoke to the pupils, the strikers themselves appealed to the Department of Bantu Education and Mr Mkhize then called a parents' meeting.

Mr Mpulo and his staff held a four-hour meeting with an interim students' committee behind closed doors yesterday morning. The meeting ended in a deadlock, and students said they planned to continue boycotting classes.

In the afternoon Mr Mkhize, was called to the school to address the children. That meeting also ended in a deadlock.

Another students' interim committee was elected and last night it met Mr Mkhize behind closed doors. The result of the meeting is not known.

In a third attempt to end the strike, the students drafted a letter, listing their grievances, to the Regional Director of Bantu Education.

A student said they wrote because they knew that school inspector Mr J P de Beer would not talk to them.

School board chairman the Rev Philemon Ngwenya also refused to discuss the controversy with them.

At yesterday's meeting in the school yard, Mr Mkhize told the children that they should go back to their classes and leave the matter for their parents to decide. He said a meeting between parents and the school committee would be held on Saturday.

Meanwhile, the strike spread to a second school in the area as about 400 Standard five and form one pupils at Belle Higher Primary, Orlando West, downed books in protest at having to do mathematics and social studies through Afrikaans.

The strike at Belle started when children walked out of classes yesterday when it was time for mathematics. They refused to return and demanded to see the chairman of the school board.

The strike at Orlando West Junior, was calmer yesterday after violent incidents on Tuesday, when students seized a tape recorder from vice-principal, Mr F Nhlapo, and threatened to beat him up.

Mr Nhlapo had to be escorted home by the principal, after students accused him of being a police informer.

The strike broke out on Monday when children refused to go to classes and demanded to be taught Mathematics and Social Studies in English.

School officials try unsuccessfully to get pupils back into the classroom, but the strike spreads to yet another school.

20 May 1976 The World

Therefore to support Paul's observation, late in May 1976 *The World* newspaper picked up the fact that our class boycott had a 'domino' effect which affected schools which faced the same problem that students at PJSS faced. Paul continues:

As I have said, most of us loitered around the school in order to maintain discipline. Seth and others like Mr Nkosi [a Form Three student who sympathised with us] would go out and drum support for us from other schools... there was no student organisation in our school, we chose our leaders and we certainly gave them the mandate to negotiate on our behalf.

June 1976

The situation was getting desperate because we were approaching June, a half-yearly exam period, and nothing was going on – we were not getting the reply

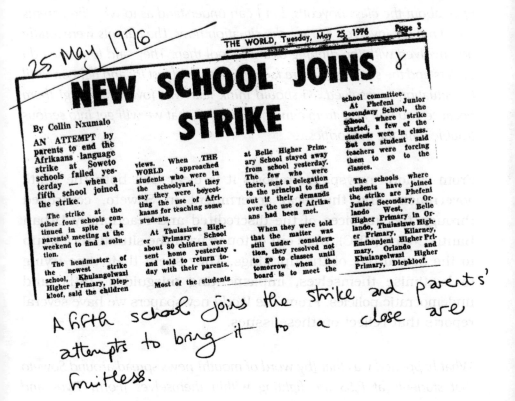

25 May 1976

THE WORLD, Tuesday, May 25, 1976   Page 3

NEW SCHOOL JOINS STRIKE

By Collin Nxumalo

AN ATTEMPT by parents to end the Afrikaans language strike at Soweto schools failed yesterday — when a fifth school joined the strike.

The strike at the other four schools continued in spite of a parents' meeting at the weekend to find a solution.

The headmaster of the newest strike school, Khulangolwazi Higher Primary, Diepkloof, said the children

views. When THE WORLD approached students who were in the schoolyard, they say they were boycotting the use of Afrikaans for teaching some students.

At Thulasizwe Higher Primary School about 80 children were sent home yesterday and told to return today with their parents.

Most of the students

at Belle Higher Primary School stayed away from school yesterday. The few who were there, sent a delegation to the principal to find out if their demands over the use of Afrikaans had been met.

When they were told that the matter was still under consideration, they resolved not to go to classes until tomorrow when the board is to meet the

school committee.

At Phefeni Junior Secondary School, the school where strike started, a few of the students were in class. But one student said teachers were forcing them to go to the classes.

The schools where students have joined the strike are Phefeni Junior Secondary, Orlando West, Belle Higher Primary in Orlando, Thulasizwe Higher Primary, Kilarney, Emthonjeni Higher Primary, Orlando and Khulangolwazi Higher Primary, Diepkloof.

A fifth school joins the strike and parents' attempts to bring it to a close are fruitless.

27

from the principal, teachers or the inspectorate... What happened was that the Form Threes were fully aware of the situation on the day-to-day basis... There was no other way but for them to join us and guide us or help us [as seniors] to get the problem sorted out. But the way things were going, they would be with us at a particular time and be on the other side at another particular time. We expected them to down their pens [and not to write their June half-yearly exams]. We wanted full sympathy from them, not a half-baked type of thing. They carried on with their studies [and began to write their June exams during the first week of June] whilst nothing was being resolved, so we decided to go inside the exam room and tore up the exam papers, and forced them out the classrooms. That is exactly when things started to get sour now – they then officially joined us because they had no option...

At home most of the parents were aware about what was happening at PJSS, about the class boycotts, but I can understand as to why the parents could not get involved as I see the situation now. The parents were totally not involved with the running of the school then. They said to us they do understand the situation we are facing, we should just try and fight on until the situation is resolved... I should think fear was [overwhelming] them because you will hear from a mother or father that we will get into serious trouble with the authorities...

From various newspaper reports it is clear that both the white government and the local government in Soweto, controlled through the auspices of the discredited and reactionary Urban Bantu Coucil (UBC), were out of touch with the situation right up to the actual day of the uprisings. They spent their time trying to legitimise themselves, implementing misguided, futile and undemocratic policies. From *The World* newspapers we have several reports that reflect on these issues.

What happened was that [by word of mouth] news spread around Soweto that students at PJSS are fighting within themselves [Form Twos and

Threes]. Other senior secondary schools like Orlando West High and Orlando High in Orlando East sent some messages saying that there should not be any fights among us. And then we had a meeting, it was on a Monday [June 14] whereby Seth addressed all of us and said that on Wednesday most of the schools in Soweto will come and assemble at our school from where we will stage a march. They [other schools] will come and assemble at our school from where we will stage a march, they will come and support the fight we are having with the Department of Bantu Education and the inspectorate and to stage a march. We will raise placards and the stuff to say to the authorities that Afrikaans as a medium of instruction should be done away with.

The march was going to be [an easy-going thing]... whereby female students will wear our trousers or their fathers' trousers and we will wear our sisters' dresses – it would be like a Guy Fawkes thing and we would go around Soweto making other statements... We laughed about the matter, we were frustrated and some students who had a sense of humour wanted us to release the tension creatively. It never turned out that way. Most of the students from other schools turned out in their full school uniforms. We did not take notice of them when they came to our school. What happened was that in other schools, when they decided to leave their premises to come and join us, the principals and the teachers in their schools did not know that the students were going to meet en masse. Teachers and principals became concerned with the situation and followed their students as their roads were leading to PJSS.

Where this school is situated you can actually see the Orlando Police Station across the railroad there. I should think that one of our teachers or the principal telephoned the police to sort of monitor the movement of the students – and the police were also amazed... It was very peaceful, nobody had a stick, stone or anything – all we wanted to do was to stage the march and then come back... We then converged at our school, then the route of the march was mapped out...

Continued on page 34

29

TUESDAY, APRIL 27, 1976

New Govt moves over teachers and language coming

By Eric Mont
Education Reporter

THE Government is to announce a new deal for Black teachers any day now — and the problem of the medium of instruction in schools is to be reviewed.

This is the hopeful message from the African Teachers' Association of South Africa (ATASA) delegation which met officials of the Bantu Education Department in Pretoria yesterday.

Members of the delegation were Messrs R L Pheteni, acting president of ATASA, H H Dlamlenze,

D M Dlephu, D D Ramneti, L T Taunyane, N Kumalo, B Mayeza, Mahlatsela and Mrs J Molobi.

The two main points for discussion at the meeting were employment conditions for teachers and the problems of the policy of the dual medium of instruction.

TALKS

Mr H H Dlamlenze, the spokesman for the delegation, said last night that the talks were well balanced and that the attitude of the Department's officials had been encouraging.

"I want to say to all our teachers that we are

hopeful that the salary announcement due in Parliament shortly will be favourable to all teachers, and especially to married and lady teachers.

"I also trust that the new regulations relating to employment and working conditions of teachers will be drawn with a sincere aim to abolish all irregularities and unnecessary difficulties.

"We need regulations which will involve teachers in their affairs instead of arbitrary decision-makers like the school boards and committees," he added.

On the question of the medium of instruction Mr Dlamlenze said the dele-

gation had been promised that the matter had been noted and would be discussed with the relevant authorities.

"We asked the Department to put aside politics and take a decision on purely professional grounds," said Mr Dlamlenze.

In its memorandum ATASA argued that the learning burden placed on young pupils was not only cruel, but contrary to the policy which claimed all Blacks belonged to some homeland. The homelands have decided to use English as the medium of instruction at post-primary schools.

The African Teachers' Association have an encouraging meeting with the Department of Bantu Education, where they discuss employment conditions and Afrikaans as medium of instruction.

30

UBC men storm out of meeting

By WILLIE BOKALA

A LARGE number of councillors last night stormed out of the Soweto Urban Council meeting called specially to discuss the controversial Afrikaans teaching issue – leaving only nine councillors to continue.

The issue was one of the hottest ever handled by the UBC.

Members of the Soweto Progressive Party led by Mr Lennox Mlonzi and makgotla under Mr Siegfried Manthata stormed out of the meeting after Mr David Thebehali threw his name plaque at Mr Leonard Mosala.

SHOUTED

The row started while Councillor Thebehali was speaking. He shouted several times that Councillor Mosala and his party keep quiet when he speaks.

When it seemed his plea fell on deaf ears, he angrily grabbed his name plaque and sent it flying across the room, over the heads of other councillors to Mr Mosala. But he missed.

Thereafter, total confusion and exchange of abusive words followed.

DELEGATION

There were also shouts of "Mr Chairman, I am not afraid of that young boy. He must be thrown out of this meeting or we walk out.

"If this meeting is going to allow such things then we are sorry we can't stand it," Mr Mlonzi said before he walked out followed by others.

However, members who stayed after the walk-out appointed a delegation of five to meet the Minister of Bantu Education and Development, Mr M C Botha on July 8. The deputation is the same that met Mr W C Ackerman, Director of Bantu Education, last week.

The deputation consists of Mr T J Makhaya, chairman, Mr Peter Lengene, Mr Richard Maponya, Mr David Thebehali and Mr Sipho Motha.

Earlier Mr Thebehali told the council that their meeting with Mr Ackerman was the most difficult and frustrating he ever attended. He said they got no co-operation from the director.

"The impression he gave me was that the issue is a professional matter and cannot be discussed with non-

professionals like us," Councillor Thebehali said.

GOVERNMENT

He said Mr Ackerman stressed that no change would be brought to schools as the policy was 50–50 and had to stay like that. Mr Ackerman also pointed out to them that nothing could be done and that schools for Black children were financed by the Government.

"He also told us that some schools had been granted permission to apply for deviation. But what surprised me was that he could not supply proof and give us the number or names of those schools," he said.

WALK OUT

Mr Makhaya told the meeting after the walk-out that he was prepared to go it alone if other councillors did not want to be involved. "I will fight the issue to the end and I must say I can do that alone. We have not come here for a showdown but to discuss our children's problems," he said.

He said an appeal would be made to children to go back to classes until the deputation had met the Minister.

Members of the Urban Bantu Council storm out of a chaotic meeting at which the Afrikaans teaching matter was discussed.

15 June 1976 The World

31

UBC men in new school row

By Collin Nxumalo and Willie Bokala

COUNCILLORS WHO stormed out of the Soweto UBC meeting called to discuss the enforcement of Afrikaans teaching in schools are not pulling out of the issue – but, they say they will not accept the "illegal" deputation appointed at Monday's meeting.

Councillors Lennox Mlonzi and Leonard Mosala said last night that they plan to see the Chief Director of the West Rand Administration Board to ask him to reject the deputation which was appointed after they and others walked out of the meeting.

"ILLEGAL"

They said that the deputation, appointed to meet the Minister of Bantu Education and Development, Mr M C Botha, was "illegal" because it was appointed at a meeting which was not properly constituted.

Councillors stormed out of the meeting – leaving only nine councillors present – after Councillor David Thebehali threw his name plaque at Mr Mosala. No decision had been taken when the councillors, members of Progressive Party led by Mr Mlonzi and of makgotla under Mr Siegfried Manthata walked out.

CONTROVERSY

Mr Mosala said other councillors were not taking the controversy seriously. "What happened at the meeting would not have happened if we were all serious about the matter. They shouldn't play around with an issue like this one.

"They have failed to realise that this is a burning issue which needs immediate attention. I doubt if we shall serve with them again after what they have done.

We were trying our best to solve our children's problems," Mr Mosala said.

Mr Mlonzi said the chairman, Mr T J Makhaya, should not have allowed the meeting to continue after that walk-out.

He said another meeting should be called immediately to continue the struggle against teaching in Afrikaans in schools.

PREPARED

"We are prepared to fight the matter but we won't stand abuse from fellow councillors," Mr Mlonzi said.

He said he was going to see Mr Manie Mulder "because the deputation appointed was not democratically elected. I will also apologise to what happened at the meeting. The procedure was to adjourn the meeting for about 15 minutes and if after that there was still no quorum, the meeting should have been called off."

UBC members storm out of the meeting. They maintain the meeting failed to realise that the Afrikaans teaching is a burning matter that needs immediate attention.

16 June 1976

32

Need for cool heads over language row

15 June 1976 — The World

THE warning by Urban Bantu Councillor, Mr Leonard Mosala, that another "Sharpeville" type incident could develop in Soweto over the controversial Afrikaans medium of instruction must be taken seriously.

As Mr Mosala points out, the presence of police on school premises tends to incite the children whose feelings are running high at the moment. On more than one occasion principals have had to appeal to police to leave the premises.

Obviously a situation like this cannot be allowed to go on indefinitely. What is needed now, more than ever, is cool heads to deal with the issues confronting our children.

What should have particularly disturbed parents is their apparent lack of control over their children. We agree entirely with Mr Mosala's analysis that many kids have lost respect for their elders. They see us as people whose dignity and pride has been hurt and who have seemingly lost the will to resist injustice.

Our children's stand suggests that they do not intend to suffer the same indignities. It should prompt a lot of soul searching among our people.

Already there are those who are beginning to respond to the challenge. Men like Dr Aaron Mathlare and his interim committee of the proposed Soweto Parents' Association have made it clear that they appreciate the plight of the Black student. They have responded by saying they as parents are not going to stand idly by while their children fight their battles.

We therefore hope that this committee will be able to rally people around the table and achieve a measure of success in defusing the tense atmosphere prevalent in Soweto.

Meanwhile, students should refrain from anything that may spark off serious trouble. In the same breath, we trust the police will act in a diplomatic manner.

As for the Department of Bantu Education, an awful lot rests on their shoulders to act responsibly in the language controversy. They must realise that forcing Afrikaans down the throats of our people can only breed resentment.

-ders

The day before the notorious uprisings of 16 June 1976, Urban Bantu Councillor warns that another 'sharpeville' incident could develop, as children's 'feelings are running high at the moment'.

In the middle of the street leading up to Maponya stores, the police came in their Landrover and blocked the street. But we were prepared to go past the police and stage the march and come back to our school. And the police said 'No, you people are not going to go past us.' That is when exactly the trouble started... The police said we must disperse in five minutes but we refused because we were not fighting anybody, but just staging a march... to get the public and parents to know about our plight and then come back to school...

We read in the newspapers that students have formed the SSRC and that the chairman was Tsietsie Mashinini. I did not know anything about Tsietsie, the person that I knew was Seth Mazibuko... We heard that the SSRC was going to co-ordinate the student activities around Soweto but now our problem was that they were not democratically elected... We only heard about it when the news was published in newspapers. The people who were affected by the Afrikaans medium of instruction issue should have been part and parcel of the organisation. But what happened was that the entire leadership was made up of people who were not affected by this issue, as they were high school students. Seth was never given the mandate to join the SSRC but was given the mandate to drum up support for us from other junior secondary schools who were also affected by this issue... We would try to meet but we had problems from the police... Other schools did not have the problem. They would go to school and discuss issues. This is what happened at Morris Isaacson, and Naledi High and all other high schools – that is how they managed to carry on [and formed the SSRC] because PJSS was closed...

We did not know then what the liberation movements were standing for. We only knew that there was an organisation called the PAC, and there was also an organisation called the ANC. The president's house in Orlando West was just near to [opposite] our school; we knew that the house belonged to Mr Mandela. We had not seen him in the newspapers or anywhere, we only knew that he was arrested and tried for treason and stuff like that. We did not exactly know the history of the ANC or the PAC, we just knew that these

34

organisations were somewhere in Zambia and we did not know what they were doing there... The BCM was not there as well, the whole initiative was taken by students, especially those at PJSS... I should think this can be rectified by people coming out and speaking the truth... I do know the whereabouts of most of the students from the various classes. Then the true reflection of the story will be told [if we hold reunions].

Verbatim Statement of Njabulo Nkonyane – December 1995 [In 1976 Mr Nkonyane was a Form Two student at Mncube Secondary School in Mofolo North, Soweto. He was 14 years old then. Njabulo Nkonyane is now a Mathematics lecturer at Vista University. He obtained his Masters in Maths in the USA.]

June 1976

No really, we were not affected. We did not have to use Afrikaans as a medium of instruction [like Morris Isaacson High School – their school was exempted from using Afrikaans as a medium of instruction]... I was aware that PJSS was using Afrikaans as a medium of instruction but it was a constant fear that we will be required to use Afrikaans as a medium of instruction [in the near future]... Actually that is a kind of a thing that made one contemplate leaving school because I just could not figure out how I would learn anything in Afrikaans. It having the kind of connotations it had as an oppressor's language and all that... I knew there was SASO [South African Students' Organisation] and I knew that there was SASM but I did not belong to any of them. I had a vague idea [about politics then]. I knew Steve Biko was a leader but beyond that I did not know... I did not know about BC [Black Consciousness] for instance, I mean as a loaded term that it turns out to be, and I mean I knew very little at that stage... I knew Mandela was a leader in prison at that time. I knew rudimentary things like that... We were aware what was happening at PJSS [class boycotts]. We sympathised at a far-off level, not at a level of taking part (given that we were not affected). We admired the courage that you people [the author and his classmates] showed you know when other schools came in like Morris Isaacson... it was a turbulent kind of thing where people are doing something and challenging the system.

There had been students' strikes before, but it seemed a whole lot that you people were challenging. One was just standing in awe, just looking in, not sure that this would be that. I could not see it coming up to 16 June for instance – I could not visualise that – nothing had prepared me for that kind of a thing. I could not think of it being national or anything. I just thought that we were students who were really bold and taking a stand and I saw it as a desperate move and I could identify with it because Afrikaans had this oppressor's image and connotations. No one would have liked to [use it as a medium of instruction]... In as far as participating in 16 June it sort of happened... it was not planned on our part – when 16 June came about, some other students [from other schools] came over to our school and we joined in the march. We knew what the issues were but it was then a sudden thing that we started sympathising, feeling that we could take action in sympathy but it was not a pre-planned thing. We did not sit down and plan that 16 June is going to be a national day... it just happened, one thing led to another and it blossomed to what it got to be... There was an article in the newspaper – The World or Post but one of those black newspapers – that actually announced that there was going to be a student demonstration on the sixteenth.

I remember that when we were at the [school] assembly that morning, the principal then, Mr Mahlaba, actually announced that other students from other schools are probably going to come here, and there was going to be this demonstration. He expected us to handle ourselves in a disciplined manner [not to join them]. But then the students came and we joined up... The demonstration took a life of its own once we were in, nobody could tell us [to toe the line]. It was not guided, things happened, police reacted the way they did. We also reacted, it had a life of its own... 16 June actually took adults by surprise. I mean nobody expected anything that big to happen from the students. They could not understand, it just blew everybody away. When people got off from work there were students all over demonstrating and the cops had come and shot people and all that stuff...

I mean to the extent that the government was insisting that there were

36

people behind the demonstration. It could not be the students. It's the kind of thing that parents could not handle either, they could not anticipate it. They were also surprised that things happened the way they did... Government has always had the fear for the liberation movements, the ANC and the PAC – mostly the ANC – then there was also the BCM – and also of course the communists, everything had to be done by the communists. I suppose that they [government] thought there were Russians behind it or something but they definitely thought it was a calculated political position taken by really astute politicians, well planned and all that stuff... At least [the government] never voiced accepting that it was a student initiative and a student directed issue you know...

I never believed that it was directed by astute politicians. Now people claim left, right and centre that they were involved. Having seen how it happened, it would take something out from the sky [to believe the politicians]. I do not believe there is anything other than the students who initiated the movement, maybe later people came in and I also think that the political [liberation] movements were taken by surprise themselves. Just like everybody else...

I was in touch with the dynamics, I know that when it [class boycotts] happened in Phefeni, there was no political organisation involved and it was not politically directed. It is only afterwards that they [liberation movements] got in on the bandwagon... I think it has to do with Tsietsie Mashinini coming from Morris Isaacson. But it does not go far enough, that is kind of like saying the student struggle started in 16 June. To me it has that kind of ring to it. I know that for weeks [prior to 16 June] it was only Phefeni that was in it and only afterwards that Morris joined. When people say everything started when Morris [Isaacson School] joined, that is not giving credit where it is due... The [16 June] march itself preceded the SSRC [which was formed on 2 August 1976]. It preceded that kind of organised movement, so even the SSRC cannot claim that they have started it either... They are the people who were influenced by the political movements. I am sure... It being an entity on its own and me not being a

Continued on page 44

Schoolchildren marching through the streets of Soweto on 16 June 1976.

Students express their anger against Afrikaans as medium of instruction.

A day after the uprisings, the government is urged to carry out a top-level commission of inquiry into the events that led to the confrontation.

Despite a highly charged situation, the Urban Bantu Council fail to form a unified front to address the educational crisis.

14 June 1976 world editorial

EDITORIALS

13

Inquiry must be held into Soweto riot

SOWETO today is a place savaged by grief and anger. Grief at the unnecessary loss of life. Anger at the insensitivity of all concerned about the rising bitterness that has surrounded the Afrikaans medium of instruction controversy.

What was at first a peaceful demonstration by school children erupted as students and police squared up to each other in confrontation. This is what we feared would happen, and this is what we have warned about all along.

Frankly we cannot see any way out of the situation other than a top-level commission of inquiry into the events of yesterday. The Government has no alternative but to appoint such a commission and get to the bottom of the disturbances.

We appealed for calm and cool heads yesterday — an appeal which we reiterate today with even greater emphasis.

We would also urge the Government to take a less uncompromising stand on the Afrikaans language issue.

Castrated bulls

PERHAPS one of the ironies of yesterday's riot in Soweto is the incredible role played by the Urban Bantu Council in the face of such an explosive issue. Instead of putting their efforts together to solve the problem, they treated us to shocking scenes, turning the Jabulani Council Chamber into a battlefield, with a name plate flying and abuse the order of the day.

What is more, when they eventually got around to appointing a delegation to see the Government on the burning issue, they engaged in debates on the legalities of such a delegation on which they could not even agree.

Indeed, talk about castrated bulls!

39

THE WORLD

OUR OWN, OUR ONLY PAPER

Telephone 27-6081 Johannesburg

Throw ideology out

JOE'S BURG

AHA! I knew it was going to happen — as it has regularly in the past and to the same pattern. Word has just reached me that the schoolkids who are on strike in Soweto schools are doing so because of the Black People's Convention.

And this, dear citizens, reportedly comes from the mouth of the Regional Director of Bantu Education — a very senior official, you will note.

This could, of course, mean one of two things: Somebody will either just decide to get tough and

close down all the schools, or the matter will simply be left, hopefully, to resolve itself.

I'm not at all surprised at this reaction. I think I have heard such claims made over and over again. Anything to do with a strike — even of factory workers — is not of the people's own doing. There are always trouble-makers who provoke innocent citizens into taking certain action. I mean, the implication has always been clear: "These people can't think for themselves. Some agitator has done it."

Now how the BPC got involved in the schools I

do not know. What I do know is simply that the BPC issued a statement in which it said the kids' problem was a national issue.

What the Department is going to do about these strikes is anybody's guess. There have been warnings, pleas, you name it, for the Department to think of the interest of the kids and throw ideology into the waste-paper basket. But, as usual, a blank was drawn.

But recently I happened to have found myself in a classroom at one school in this burg. On the blackboard were notes

— history notes — in Afrikaans. Now I am no genius in the Afrikaans language, but I do believe, modesty aside, that I have a working knowledge of the 'taal' — how else can you account for the "D" I got last time out at school?

ERRORS

Now what appeared on that blackboard was a complete abortion of the language. What worried me, however, is that if the teacher could make such errors, what is expected of the kids who are supposed to learn from that teacher?

Which explains why bo-

dies like the African Teachers' Association of South Africa have appealed to the Department and pointed out that very few teachers are proficient in teaching subjects like science, maths and history in Afrikaans.

The regional director of Bantu Education allegedly believes that the striking Soweto pupils were incited by the Black People's Convention. Possibly he believes: 'Anything to do with a strike — even of factory workers — is not of the people's own doing.'

40

Schoolchildren gather to protest on 16 June 1976, while the police look on.

THE WORLD, Thursday, June 17, 1976

Riot – Kruger speaks

THE MINISTER of Justice and of Police, Mr Jimmy Kruger, last night issued a statement in Parliament on the riot in Soweto: The statement said:

'Student unrest over dissatisfaction with their curriculum has brewing in Soweto for the past ten days.

At about 8.15 am on Wednesday about 10 000 pupils launched rowdy processions. They were aggressive, screamed inciting slogans, carried banners and attacked the police who were present, as well as private vehicles and threw stones at them.

Two vehicles of the West Rand Administration Board were overturned and a White man and a Black man were chopped to death.

Two police dogs were chopped to death and set alight. Ten police vehicles were damaged and several policemen injured.

The vehicles of four White women who work in the area were badly damaged. The women were injured and admitted to hospital.

Various buildings and cards were set alight. The police tried everything to get the rioters under control and eventually were forced to fire warning shots over their heads.

Police are trying to force the students out of the residential area into an open area and to bring the situation under control.'

Minister of Justice and of Police makes
a charged statement to parliament
about the uprising of the preceding
day, 16 June 1976.

41

An estimated ten thousand Soweto schoolchildren assembled to protest and march on 16 June 1976.

THE WORLD, Friday, June 18, 1976

Botha defends language rule

SUBJECTS are taught in "English only" at seven of the senior secondary schools in Soweto which took part in demonstrations against Afrikaans as a medium of instruction, the Minister of Bantu Education, Mr M C Botha, said last night.

Only one high school offered one subject – history up to Form Three – through the medium of Afrikaans.

"The alleged aversion to Afrikaans as a medium can hardly be the only reason for the demonstrations," the Minister said in a lengthy statement defending the 50-50 language requirement.

His department had certain responsibilities to consider in its approach to medium of instruction and could not simply accede to policy by "popular request".

● The equal treatment of the two official languages as entrenched in the constitution.

● The predominance of one official language over the other changed from region to region.

"Introduction of one of the languages as sole medium of instruction would adversely affect the region where the other language predominates."

● The introduction of a "foreign language" as medium in the primary school was a backward step educationally with which the department would not like to be associated: Concept formation and understanding at this stage takes place best through the vernacular.

The Minister of Bantu Education, states that in seven of the schools that demonstrated against Afrikaans as medium of instruction, subjects are taught in English only.

42

Kids told — get back to school

Tsietsie Mashinini pictured after a meeting of students at Morris Isaacson High School, Soweto, yesterday. He was elected chairman of the new Soweto Students' Representative Council.

by DUMA NDLOVU

SOWETO STUDENTS were yesterday urged to go back to school and solve their problems from within.

Parents and students said this at a three hour meeting called by Soweto's Black Parents' Association yesterday.

The meeting was attended by more than 200 parents and students and was intended to solve problems arising from the present situation in Soweto schools.

Tsietsie Mashinini, a matric student at Morris Isaacson, who is the regional president of the South African Students' Movement and chairman of the body representing students in matters concerning the present rift, urged students to go back to school today so that a solution could be found.

"We can only conquer when we have a strong standpoint and stand as one."

He also said the students were going to meet at Morris Isaacson High School this morning and discuss what was to be done.

He urged all junior secondaries and high schools to send two representatives to the meeting, to start at 9 am.

UNITE

Another student, Murphy Morobe, urged fellow students to unite.

Mr Clarence Mlokoti, principal of the Daliwonga Secondary School in Dube, called on parents to consider the problems of the students.

"Our future today is being determined by the students. That is why we have to consider them. We should meet them and get to know their programme and then work alongside them," he said.

Police action was strongly criticised.

PROTEST

At the end of the meeting the parents and students were called upon by Dr Manas Buthelezi, chairman of the BPA, to make resolutions.

Some of the points which arose were:

- The immediate release of all detained students. (It was also stated that although the Minister of Justice, Mr Jimmy Kruger, had given an assurance to this effect students were still being detained.)
- The total scrapping of the Bantu Education system.
- Members of the BPA, SASM, and all other Black organisations, parents and students, to march together in protest against the arrests of students.

Soweto's Black Parents' Association urges pupils to go back to school at a meeting of over 200 pupils and parents.

2 August 1976

43

member of it, anything could have happened. I would accept that the BCM people came to the SSRC and offered direction or the ANC, whoever, that probably happened but it was after [the major events in June].

A whole lot of people who were involved, who actually lived during the era are around. And I mean it is actually not so long that people do not remember. I think if one intends bringing the truth about the matter you can talk to enough people. One can write or put it in some kind of media then it would debunk the myth that [16 June protest] was initiated by communists or whoever... I think that it is a common thread in people's history that after a while, people make claims and after a while these claims become a reality and everybody accepts that as a truth. Even people who knew what really happened, they just accept it. They would not take time to argue the thing. They would accept that [myth] either as a non-issue or even they would start to repeat the thing [myth as reality]... When we actually put questions to them it is then they would step back and say it really did not happen that way. That is why I would think that if nobody corrected things eventually it would be an accepted fact that it was an ANC initiative. It used to be the BCM. Now that the BCM is in tatters, it is the ANC who are saying they did it [initiated the students' protest]. So eventually everybody will believe that it is their responsibility.

Like any 14-year-old, we were naive but the situation forced us to mature much faster than we would have, facing bullets everyday of your life, tear-gas just about all the time. I remember we use to joke that if we have not smelled or seen teargas for a week, something was wrong – breathing clean air for two days. Things like that made one mature very quickly. We started reading books, we got politicised almost overnight and I think because of that, students played an invaluable role. People who claim that they did things on behalf of the students [should know that] those things could not happen had the students not reached political maturity. Hence I am certain that students took up a strong political role... We decided then we would never go back to school, we would boycott Bantu Education henceforth... I went to [Sached-Turret Correspondence College] and you [the author] went there too because we boycotted Bantu Education. We started studying the British General Certificate of Education [GCE] as an alternative...

Analysing the above chronology of events as spelled out by the two informants it is apparent that, first, if the students at Phefeni Junior Secondary School had not been tenacious with their class boycotts that took place in May, and gave up like other students from various schools, then the most important turning-point in our country's history might have been delayed and this includes our liberation. Secondly, the uprisings were not 'spontaneous', as the students from PJSS were on a go-slow as early as in March 1976. Thirdly, liberation movements, and student organisations like SASO and SASM, played no significant role either in the day-to-day major debates in the classrooms or in planning the actual day of protest that involved most of the schools in Soweto. Therefore, these movements cannot rightfully claim to have organised the 1976 uprisings, precisely because the major issues at stake affected students in the classroom, not liberation nor political movements like the then unbanned BCM.

Because commemorations can be contested[4], unlike Nozipho Diseko[5] and others, I am of the opinion that the contributions of the liberation movements and other students' organisations to the major discussions and actual events prior to 16 June 1976 are debatable. Johnson, Kane-Berman, Hyslop and Brewer regard the SASM as an extension of the BCM. It represented the latter in schools, whilst Hirson, Brickhill and Brooks refer to obscure links between the SASM and the ANC. But Diseko takes this last point further as she argues that the SASM was formed in 1968 prior to the formation of the BCM [and AZAPO] in the 1970s. She goes on to argue that in its infancy, this organisation adhered to no particular ideology, but when Black Consciousness emerged in the 1970s it was embraced as its philosophy.

45

However, by the end of 1974 dissatisfaction with the limitations of BC led to the establishment of formal ties with the ANC and the 1976 uprising consolidated this change, which was largely unnoticed then by the state and other political formations. Therefore to some extent Diseko argues that the ANC was instructive in the events that led to the 1976 uprisings as she believes that the SASM was instrumental in organising the student uprisings.

In putting forward my counter-memories as a 14-year-old Form Two student at PJSS in Soweto I argue that it is these students [including Form Ones] themselves who were the actual champions of their own struggles, and very young students indeed. They had never heard of the SASM or SASO, nor were they aware of these organisations' role in student politics then. They – in fact, I too, for I was one of them – had not joined any student movement and had not developed intellectually to understand complex theoretical paradigms involving the ANC, PAC, liberation theory or Black Consciousness. This is besides the fact that we were 'vaguely' aware of our status as oppressed people. And again, President Mandela's Orlando West matchbox house, which was opposite PJSS, played a symbolic role as it constantly reminded us of our plight as oppressed people. It is necessary to locate student protests within broader contexts, as Diseko has done in her research, including her University of Oxford doctoral thesis. But this becomes problematic if the efforts of young, ordinary students are subsumed under the dominant liberation theory or movement of that particular time in history and if this research is done at the expense of day-to-day student experiences and other influences that existed within the schools and classrooms.

As late as December 1976, the liberation movements were desperately clamouring for the support of the large number of

46

ANC-PAC ENLIST EXILED STUDENTS

THE BATTLE is on outside South African hearts and minds of the more than 1 000 students who fled the country following the unrests.

In Tanzania, both the African National Congress and the Pan-Africanist Congress are vieing with each other to enlist the young exiles.

Reporting from Dar es Salaam, in Tanzania, The Christian Science Monitor claims officials of the ANC and rival PAC – both banned in South Africa – are travelling all over Southern Africa trying to enlist the fleeing students.

It cannot be determined how many of the exiles have already joined one of the two organisations, who believe armed struggle is the only way of liberating the Black man in South Africa.

But a PAC spokesman in

by WORLD REPORTER

Tanzania claimed that 200 of the students had already joined them. He refused to say where the students were, or to allow them to be interviewed.

Enrolled

An ANC official claimed his organisation had enrolled 80 youths in Tanzania alone. Some were already in guerrilla training camps in Southern Tanzania, he said.

According to the Christian Science Monitor, the ANC appears to be shepherding its new recruits towards training to infiltrate back into South Africa with weapons.

Probably as a result of this body's ties with the Soviet Union and Mozambique it seems more militarily advanced than the PAC.

● At the same time

Western sources have claimed most of the students leaving South Africa are refusing to join either the ANC or PAC, preferring to stick to their own organisations – SASO and SASM (the South African Students Movement).

However, students who land in Tanzania are compelled to join either the PAC or ANC. This is not the case in Swaziland, Lesotho or Botswana.

At present there are estimated to be at least 600 students in Botswana alone, and the country is struggling to support them. An appeal has already been made to the Organisation of African Unity for help.

In its report, the Monitor claims all three exiled students it interviewed in Tanzania said they would rather continue with their education than train as guerrillas.

Over 1 000 South African students in exile are being recruited by the ANC and PAC, but some prefer to remain members of existing South African organisations.

30 December 1976 The World

students who went into exile. As they were caught by surprise and were underprepared by this exodus of a large number of students, they cannot claim that they were instructive in organising the June uprisings.

In fact, initially the students went into exile looking for a symbolic 'home' in the various camps, since they were not recruited by the liberation movements, their reception was chaotic in most cases. There were various splinter groups which came into place within the liberation movements. Their major aim was to win the hearts and minds of this new, highly radical but politically immature support base. The different factions also wanted to push their own agendas for leadership within these movements. As soon as students recognized this and the tension caused by their presence, they set up their own organisations in exile. One can argue that the ANC managed to regroup and rise above factionalism. The PAC, however, was never able to recover and one suspects that its poor showing in the present-day South African political scene has internal dynamics which can be traced back to this era.

Themba Molefe, a political correspondence for the *Sowetan* newspaper, provides us with the following chronology and background to the events prior to 16 June 1976 upon which I base my counter-memories. This also includes his article based on eye-witness accounts from the *Sowetan* archives[6].

THE SOWETAN, Friday, June 16, 1995

This is what led to the '76 riots...

By Themba Molefe
Political Correspondent

In 1974 the Southern Transvaal regional department of Bantu Education issued a directive that Afrikaans be a medium of instruction in black junior secondary schools – on a 50-50 basis with English.

This generated widespread protests from teacher organisations and school boards inside and outside Soweto.

Educationists saw the directive as a contradiction to a statement made the previous year by the then Secretary for Bantu Education, the late Dr H J van Zyl, who had made it clear that the medium of instruction in schools should be decided by the individual school boards in consultation with himself personally.

He had stated that it was not in the interests of the pupils to have two mediums of instruction.

This is what happened:

• Following the 50-50 language directive in late 1974, school boards and teacher organisations made representations to the Minis-ter of Bantu Education Mr C Botha for a decision against this policy. This was turned down.

• In May 1975 the joint northern and southern Trans-vaal school boards elected a committee to take up the issue again with the Department of Bantu Education.

• The committee subsequently had at least one meeting with Van Zyl but returned home dissatisfied.

• During 1975 several school boards ordered their schools to ignore the language instruction and teach in English only.

• At several secret meetings the school boards were told in no uncertain terms to toe the line of the Department of Bantu Education. Most school boards relented.

• In February 1976 the dispute surfaced when two members of the Meadowlands Tswana School Board in Soweto were fired by the Regional Director of Bantu Education, Mr W C Ackerman.

The entire school board resigned in sympathy.

• Soweto secondary school pupils then took the matter up on May 17 1976 when the Form One (Std 6) and Form Two (Std 7) pupils refused to attend classes until their demands to have the Afrikaans order withdrawn were met.

• Within a week three schools had joined the Phefeni Junior Secondary in boycotting classes. Already, about 1 600 pupils had been affected.

At that stage the Bantu Education inspectorate responsible for those schools refused to get involved saying

the policy had been laid down by the Government.

• By the end of May 1976 seven schools involving more than 2 000 pupils had joined the strike but many later returned to classes. Only the Phefeni pupils were left sticking to their boycott.

• By Monday 14 June 1976 plans for a massive pupil demonstration were heard of.

After consistently refusing to even consider hearing black parents and teacher representation on the issue, Deputy Minister of Bantu Education Dr Andries Treurnicht told Parliament: "Why should blacks be allowed in schools if they do not want to be taught in the language chosen by the Government?

"The Afrikaners were also forced by the English to learn their language."

On June 15 1976 Soweto awoke to find schools teaming with police.

A councillor in the then Urban Bantu Council, Mr Leonard Mosala, warned that another "Sharpeville" could occur in Soweto over the enforcing of Afrikaans as a medium of instruction.

On 16 June the United Nations Security Council demanded answers after hearing that South African Police bullets had claimed the lives of 40 unarmed school children.

In 1995, a modern political correspondent reflects on the events leading up to the 1976 uprisings.

16 June 1995

Sowetan

49

Part Two: Remembrance as a contested activity

How do the various liberation movements and political parties commemorate 16 June? Because remembrance is a contested activity, controversy over how to commemorate the Soweto uprisings is self-evident[7]. The state proclaimed official commemoration of the uprisings to take effect from 1995, nineteen years after the actual event (on 16 June 1976). This day is now a public holiday: Youth Day. It has moved from being labelled literally and figuratively, a 'black' day, to a 'colour-blind' Youth Day. At a minimum, the definition of the event is the centre of a struggle: what and whose stories are worth remembering in relation to the event under consideration? As well, what it means to learn from the past given in the present, or what it might mean to learn about our present given our social organization of representations of the past.

The literature that discusses the origins of the Soweto uprising regards the various liberation movements as the driving force that fanned the flames, or the motor that drove the protesting students. Every year, prior to the commemoration of 16 June 1976, one becomes aware of the dogfight between various liberation movements clamouring and posturing for recognition as champions of the uprisings. This is because this day is recognised as the most important turning point in our country's history.

One has to look at the various newspapers and media representations of the commemoration events. These movements tell us endless stories about their underground preparations and how they laid the ground for the students through their internal and

50

external cells, preparing them for that fateful day, 16 June 1976. The main protagonists in this regard were the then unbanned Black Consciousness Movement, AZAPO, the banned PAC and the ANC. The various authors of academic literature mention only two students' organisations, namely the South African Students Movement and the South African Student Organisation. But in most analyses both students' organisations are subsumed and regarded as surrogates of the BCM political tradition with SASM operating in both secondary and high schools and SASO in black universities[8]. All of this points to the construction of hegemonic memories which, most often through what they omit, suppress remembrances which might call into question existing forms of social and knowledge production and the distribution of material wealth.

Before the general elections in South Africa of April 1994, the state as a dominant group used, among other things, coercive means to maintain social control. This control was not completely effective because it was opposed and overcome by surbodinate groups like the trade unions and student movement. But other sites of struggle between these groups involved the production of popular memory. Taken together, these sites form the field within which the practice of historical representation takes place, including the locus of the social production of collective memory through commemorations. Simons[9] identifies the following sites:

> Government rituals concerning national origins; literally the theatre of the state, eg the traditions of parliament and monarchy. State-sponsored commemorations either declared or enacted in law, eg holidays or national day of remembrance.
>
> National and local archives which not only select what is considered important to preserve but define the retrieval

51

codes which provide access to stored documents and arte-
facts.

Public and private schools which mediate the relation
between communities and state-sanctioned historical representations. Academic journals and books. Fiction and non-
fiction, adult and children's books produced for the public.
Newspapers, magazines and television news programmes
and documentaries. Fictional narratives produced for either
television or cinema. Museum and galleries, both state-
sponsored and private.

Prints, posters, postcards and T-shirts, photo albums and
diaries, collections of memorabilia. Story quilts and apparels.
Performance spaces; theatre, community centres etc, public
art ranging from state-commissioned monuments to community murals. Orally produced and reproduced family or
community narratives, and ritualised expressive speech forms.

Before the elections in April 1994, the liberation movements used
some of these sites to commemorate the Soweto uprisings. They
used these sites to great effect to mould historical and national
consciousness among black people[10]. This is because history had
come to be seen as an important oppositional tool in the country's political culture. As an example we had all liberation movements emphasizing the resistance put up by black students in
1976 to oppression. This was done by using popular memories of
the 1976 generation who had by then affiliated to the different
liberation movements, United Democratic Front and trade unions.
Some of them, like Murphy Morobe, had leadership positions
within these organisations.

But these commemorations were a highly contested terrain, as
they still are today. They were held at different venues and

according to political affiliation, as is still the case today. During these services various memories and counter-memories are presented. What has become apparent is that the ANC has shifted its position, as it no longer uses these commemorations to emphasize resistance put up by black societies during the apartheid years. Their focus now is on national reconciliation and nation-building. This was quite apparent in President Mandela's gesture towards the Springboks national rugby team at a 1995 Youth Day rally held at Ezakheni Township, in KwaZulu-Natal. This event was reported in various media which did not miss the opportunity to mention that he was wearing a Springbok sports cap. The *Saturday Star*[11] reported that he urged youthful supporters to back the Springboks – whom he described as 'our kind'. It is also reported that he made a special plea to youth to co-operate with the once-hated police. The Springbok captain, Francois Pienaar returned the gesture and commented: 'To have your own President wearing a Springbok hat in the townships and telling the people to back the Springboks is a tremendous feeling'.[12]

Both the PAC and AZAPO had explicit political messages to deliver on this day. They chided the Government of National Unity for treating this day with contempt and disrespect as a pop concert was arranged in Mmabatho on Youth Day 1995. It was reported in some newspapers that fighting broke out amongst the fans and those injured were hospitalised. They clamoured to see pop music idol Rebecca Molope and not, it seemed, to hear their political heroes on Youth Day.

Not only was the occasion inappropriate, but people behaved badly too. The PAC and AZAPO asked the following questions: Do Jews attend festive functions when they remember their people who perished under Hitler? Do Christians celebrate in a manner unbecoming on Good Friday?[13] AZAPO further announced its campaign for the exhumation and reburial in South Africa of all who died outside the country during the liberation struggle.

Conclusion

Societies differ in the degree to which their citizens can contest the hegemonic practices of commemoration. In democratic communities we at least acknowledge in principle that previously established commemorative practice should be open to critique and contention. Thus democracy entails an ongoing tension between retaining affirmed shared memories and preserving the possibility that such memories can be opened to contestation. In other words, most democrats cherish, rather than dismiss, the practice of counter-memory. This calls into question both the social imagination previously secured by particular commemorations as well as the social interests and ethical visions supported by such imaginations. This practice involves a process of self-criticism and a renewal of identity. Therefore possibilities are opened for change in the basic terms of reference, in the way citizens, their environment and their state relate to each other. Such a process does not mean mindlessly accepting all contesting counter-memories. It does mean learning how to hear what people (individuals as well as groups) assert and seriously considering the claim they make on our understanding of the present[14.] This is very important because commemorations are critical for the construction of national, group or individual identities.

End notes

1 'Pass one pass all' was a slogan adopted by protesting students in the late 1980s and early 1990s. It meant that students wished to pass and be promoted to the next level, regardless of their academic performance. Unlike the students who adopted 'pass one pass all', the 1976 generation believed in meritocracy.

2 This statement refers to the now deceased Tsietsie Mashinini, who was to become the leader of the Soweto Students' Representative Council. It was formed early in August 1976, one and a half months after the uprisings started.

3 See also the *Saturday Star*, 17 June 1995. Look at the article on Morris Isaacson High School (incorrectly referred to as a secondary school) by Tefo Mothibeli and the picture of the Gauteng MEC for education, Mary Metcalfe paying a visit to this school.

4 See John Qwelane's article in the *Saturday Star*, 17 June 1995. This article proposes that Melville Edelstein, the first white man to die in the 16 June 1976 conflagration should be remembered as well. Edelstein, a welfare worker, died near Phefeni Junior Secondary School, not long after Hector Peterson, the first victim of the uprisings, was shot and killed by the police. See also end notes 2 and 3. See also an interview of Edelstein's wife and two daughters in the same newspaper, page 5.

5 N Diseko, 'The origins and Development of the South African Student Movement [SASM]: 1968-1976', *Journal of African Studies*, Vol 1, 18, 1992, pp. 40-62. See J D Brewer, *After Soweto: an unfinished journey*, Oxford, Clarendon Press, 1986; J Hyslop, 'Social conflicts over African education in South Africa from the 1940s to 1976', PhD thesis, Witwatersrand University, 1990; J Brickhill and A Brooks, *Whirlwind Before the Storm: The origins and the development of the uprisings in Soweto and the rest of South Africa from June to December 1976*, London International Defence and Aid Fund for Southern Africa, 1980; B Hirson, *Year of Fire, year of Ash – The Soweto Revolts: Roots of a revolution?* London, Zed, 1979; J Kane-Berman, *Soweto –*

Black revolt white reaction, Johannesburg, 1978; S Johnson, *South Africa: No turning back*, London, Macmillan, 1988.

6   *Sowetan*, Friday, 16 June 1995.

7   Other important and controversial events in our history are the Day of Reconciliation (Dingaan's Day and previously Day of the Vow – 16 December) and the commemoration of the Sharpeville shootings (which took place on 21 March 1960). See also the various reports of the Sharpeville commemoration from national newspapers concerning the stand-off between the PAC and ANC supporters over the commemoration service at Sharpeville in March 1995. The Day of the Vow no longer exists, as it has been now replaced by an official holiday interestingly called Reconciliation Day.

8   See end note 4.

9   R I Simons, 'Forms of insurgency in the production of popular memories: The Columbus quincentenary and the pedagogy of counter-commemoration', *Cultural Studies 7 (1)*, 1993, pp. 73-88. He further notes that this field is homogenous as some sites incorporate a capability for reaching far more people than others. Furthermore, not all citizens have equal access to use the sites thus creating a situation in which certain groups or agencies defined by particular communities of interest have control of commemorative practices enabling certain memories and forms of remembrance to become dominant across a public sphere.

10 These organisations did not have access to sites which were able to reach far more people, like broadcast television and radio. They tended to use more marginal sites of representations, (like posters and T-shirts) which had considerable accessibility and greater potential for becoming living memories in people's every-day lives.

11 *Saturday Star,* 17 June 1995.

12 *Sowetan*, 19 June 1995. The next day the Springboks appeared on the front page of the daily *Star* newspaper holding a banner

of Masakhane, a government-funded project to kickstart development of black areas which was initiated by President Mandela.
13 *City Press* editorial page, 18 June 1995 and the *Sowetan*, 19
June 1995, p. 9. The *City Press* editorial further lambasted the
film *Sarafina*, and 'people who, up to this day, cannot sing *Nkosi
Sikelela iAfrika* and unpatriotic fools who still show disrespect
when this moving hymn is sung'.
14 R I Simon, op. cit. Still on this theme see D Cohen, *The
Combing of History*, Chicago, 1994, Chapter 7; 'The trouble
with Columbus', *Time*, 7/10/1991; F Fernandes-Armesto,
'Columbus – Hero or Villain', *History Today*, May 1992. For
controversies in South Africa see end note 2 and: J Naidoo,
'Was the Retief-Dingane treaty a fake?', *History in Africa*, 12,
1985, pp. 187-210; A Grundlingh and H Shapiro, 'From
Feverish Festival to Repetitive Ritual? The changing fortunes
of Great Trek mythology in an industrialising South Africa,
1938-1988', paper presented at the Social Transformation
Seminar, University of the Witwatersrand, Johannesburg, 17
March 1989; B J Liebenberg, 'Bloedrivier en Gods Hands',
South African Historical Journal, 12, 1980, pp. 1-12, 'Mites
rondom Bloedrivier en die Gelofte', *South African Historical
Journal*, 20, 1988, pp. 17-32; F A van Jaarsveld, 'A historical
mirror of Blood River', in A Koning and H Kearie (eds.), *The
Meaning of History*, Pretoria, 1980; A du Toit, 'No chosen
people: The myth of the Calvinist origins of Afrikaner
nationalism and racial ideology', *American Historical Review*,
88, 1983, pp. 920-952; I H Hofmeyer, 'Popularising history:
the case of Gustav Preller', unpublished seminar paper,
African Studies Institute, Witwatersrand University, August
1987; T D Moodie, *The rise of Afrikanerdom: Power, Apartheid
and the Afrikaner civil religion*, Berkeley, 1975; D O'Meara,
*Volkskapitalisme: Class, capital and ideology in the develop-
ment of Afrikaner nationalism 1934-1948*, Johannesburg,
1983; I Wilkins and H Strydom, *The Super-Afrikaners*,

Johannesburg, 1978; Hendrik Cloete, *History of the Great Boer Trek and the Origin of the South African Republics*, London, 1898. The French Revolution (including the storming of the Bastille) is another issue which is highly contested. This event is commemorated on 14 July in France. See also my manuscript on the counter-commemoration of 'Dingaan's Day' by black South Africans in the twentieth century. Look for it in the April/May 1998 issue of the *South African Historical Journal*.